## SHOP COOK EAT

# OUTSIDE Of The BOX

*with* CHRISETTA MOSLEY

Copyright © 2012 by Chrisetta Mosley

All rights reserved, including the right to reproduce the book or portions thereof in any form whatsoever.


Design by Chrisetta Mosley
Cover Photo by Cari Hachmann
Cover Design by Adam Sonnek


Printed in United States of America
by Minuteman Press of Vancouver, WA


First Edition

*For Veronica*
In Food and In Health

# ACKNOWLEDGMENTS

This book would not be possible without the help and support of many.

First and foremost, all glory and honor to God for His gifts and blessings.

An extra-special thanks to **Veronica Brock** for thinking of me to author this cookbook, her support and unwavering belief in me.

**Jeanne Hoff** for her meticulous editing and her constructive, timely feedback.

**Stephen Nelson** who helped me edit my first cookbook, *Bringing Cooking Back* and gladly stepped in for my sophomore effort. "Do what you can."

The **Health & Physical Education Department** of **Clark College**.

**Robert Knight**, President of **Clark College**.

**Lisa Borho** for welcoming me to **Clark College**.

**Clark College Bookstore** for selling *Bringing Cooking Back* and this book too. **Marti Earhart** for being a crusader in health.

**Clark College Library** for putting my cookbooks in circulation.

**Britany Martin** for capturing the food, the laughter, and moi with her lens.

**Sherri McMillan** for leading by example. Oh, and of course for writing the foreword.

**The Columbian and Live Well** for putting my words in print.

**New Seasons Market** An extra-special thanks to the **Fisher's Landing** store and **Leeann O'Neil** for getting my first little cookbook *Bringing Cooking Back* on the shelves. **Seth Hollingsworth** for planting the seed to help me get my tomato soup in the deli. **Todd** and **Peter**, the chefs for making the soup with fresh ingredients.

**Chuck's Produce & Street Market** for providing a beautiful kitchen for my cooking classes and photo shoots.

**Cascade Park Community Library** for opening their doors to me and **Teresa Torres** for helping me through them.

**Fort Vancouver Regional Library** for assigning my first Dewey Decimal number.

The staff of **Minuteman Press**, Vancouver, Washington for jumping in mid-production and getting the job done.

**Steve Oglesby** for his go-get attitude. **Adam Sonnek** for designing the cover and his countless design ideas.

**Jasmyn** my daughter, the reason I do everything I do. Mama loves you more than words can say.

**Mama** for her unconditional love and support again and again.
**Daddy** for his spiritual guidance.
**Nathan "Uncle Carlton" Mosley** for having my back and front.
**Cassie Hill** for her fresh eyes and angles.
My **Entire Family** for everything.
**Carmen** You were right, I am not suppose to work a traditional job.
**Katina** for lighting my fire to write *Bringing Cooking Back* and being my No. 1 fan.
**Tia** for always being there.
**Georgena** No matter the distance we're always close.
**Laura** Thanks for being my Gayle, the friend that everybody deserves.
**Rebecca** for believing the glass is always half full.
**Jeannine** for freeing my mind.
**Jolene George** for not giving me permission to do less than my best.
**Patricia** for her lovely spirit.
**G. Garvin, Barefoot Contessa, Martha Stewart, Sam Stern,** and **Mark Bittman** for inspiring my culinary creativity.
If *Bringing Cooking Back* would have had an acknowledgment section these folks would have been in it: **Cari Hachmann, Steve Schorr, Linda Schorr,** and **Tami** and **Nena Williams.**
To **everyone** who purchased *Bringing Cooking Back*.
The best **blog followers.** This has been an amazing journey and you've been with me every step and blog of the way.
My **cooking class regulars** at **Chuck's Produce & Street Market** you helped make this cookbook a reality.
**Clark College Penguins** for starting the Shopping, Cooking, Eating: Outside of the Box movement.

# CONTENTS

| | |
|---|---|
| FOREWORD | 9 |
| INTRODUCTION | 10 |
| WHY COOK? | 15 |
| GROCERY SHOPPING & PLANNING | 18 |
| BASICS | 30 |
| SNACKS | 42 |
| MAKE IT FAST | 54 |
| BREAKFAST | 64 |
| FARMER'S MARKET | 76 |
| SOUP & SALAD | 88 |
| CLASSICS | 104 |
| DIP & SPREADS | 110 |
| SWEET SENSATIONS | 120 |
| CREDITS | 128 |
| INDEX | 130 |

# FOREWORD

We know from experience, at Northwest Personal Training that at least half the battle in terms of someone losing weight and achieving optimal health is their nutrition. But people are busy and are often looking for the quick fix and wind up making poor choices. Chrisetta knows first hand the struggle with weight loss but she has figured out an eating plan that is simple, effective and allows someone to lose weight, feel great and achieve their personal best. She herself has lost 170 pounds adopting these nutrition, shopping and cooking concepts into her own life. It works and she's the testimony to how much your entire life can be dramatically changed when you take the time to take care of yourself. She will teach you techniques that you can adopt into your life immediately and as a result, you entire life will be positively impacted – physically, emotionally, and mentally.

**— Sherri McMillian,** M.Sc. *is the owner of Northwest Personal Training in Vancouver, Washington. Sherri has been inspiring the world to adopt a fitness lifestyle for over 20 years and has authored several books and won numerous awards.*

# INTRODUCTION

Everything about this cookbook is "Outside of the Box," including my journey and how I came to author it. I invite you to read this introduction where I share a little about myself and the inspiration behind the book.

I'm a product, and now a survivor, of childhood obesity. At my heaviest, I tipped the scales at a whopping 388 pounds. At the time, I was a single mother of an eight year old daughter and was earning a bachelor's degree from Seattle University (SU).

My experience at SU changed my life and saved my life. At 388 pounds it took an enormous effort to walk the hilly campus — aching knees, struggling to breathe while I walked. Then once in the classroom, overwhelmed by the youthful intellects that filled the room. They were running circles around me intellectually and physically. In the hallways, they were taking stairs two at a time while I waited for the elevator to go one flight. In class, the humiliation of not being able to fit into attached desk-chairs was compounded by being afraid to speak up because I felt my ideas were less than important and not so intelligent. SU is a private Catholic school. Most of the students there had been attending private schools their entire lives. Me, well, I went to a public high school umpteen years prior and transferred from a community college at the age of 28. I was new to the culture, the learning environment, and to critical thinking.

There was the feeling of shame; but while attending SU I always felt like I was under a dark cloud, in a daze. In retrospect, the highly caloric, sugary, processed boxed foods I was eating kept me feeling drugged and crappy. It's no wonder I didn't have a lot of energy or enthusiasm. The good thing that came of all of this, was the more I grew intellectually the more I became intolerant of obesity. For the first time ever, I believed I could change, had the right to change, and the courage to do it.

Fast forward, 2012: To date, I've lost 170 pounds. I've done this by making conscious food choices, preparing my meals at home and exercising regularly.

A healthy lifestyle for me begins at home in my kitchen. Cooking at home allows me to be in control of my food and what I eat. I love food and unlike a drug or alcohol problem with food you have to still use. In this case, eat. So, over the years, I've had to re-examine the way I think about food, how I interact with food, and most importantly how I prepare food. Today, I lovingly prepare 99 percent of my meals at home using fresh, whole ingredients.

I share my passion for food and cooking with others through my blog, Farewell Fatso! and by teaching cooking classes. Blogging and teaching others how to create good healthy meals brings me great joy, but I had a desire to offer more of myself. I wanted to share my enthusiasm and zeal for life by helping people transform themselves. In the fall of 2011, I enrolled in the Fitness Trainer program at Clark College in Vancouver, Washington.

Again, education was a catalyst for my growth. I was taking Health 100: Food and Your Health taught by Veronica Brock. Being a food enthusiast this class quickly became my favorite. It was more than just what to eat or not to eat. It was about how food related to my health, nourished my body, and something that I became particularly interested in -- how food and nature are connected.

Inspired by my blog followers, teaching cooking classes, and the information I was learning in Health 100, I authored my first cookbook *Bringing Cooking Back*. Veronica, of course, knew about the cookbook and even bought a copy. Our relationship continued to blossom even after the quarter was over. I was thrilled months later when Veronica called asking me for recipe ideas that could be used in Clark's curriculum, and honored when Clark's health department asked me to author this cookbook.

In creating *Shop, Cook, Eat: Outside of the Box* I want to help you re-connect to food, to truly appreciate food. I hope to inspire you to be mindful while shopping, cooking, and eating. As you shop for berries, go ahead pick them up and smell them. As you prepare grains run your fingers through them, become familiar with the texture. Relish the beauty and the aroma of the freshly roasted peppers you pull out of your oven. When you sit down to eat, take your time -- enjoy the meal, enjoy the experience. Maybe even take a moment to pay homage to those who were instrumental in bringing the food to your plate.

I truly hope that the sections of this book will allow you to celebrate every aspect of food preparation from shopping to savoring the meal you made. For this reason, I chose to include a section on Grocery Shopping and Planning that will help you easily locate the food in your store and help you stock your fridge and pantry. You'll also find a section on basic recipes that will help you whip up a healthy meal in a flash: Beans, Whole Grains, Tomato Sauce, Olive Oil Drizzle, Vegetable Stock, Vinaigrettes, Perfect Hard-Cooked Eggs.

The recipes in this book focus on using fresh, whole ingredients and are centered around simple, everyday foods that you can find in the supermarket: Wheat berries, quinoa, lentils, chickpeas, kale to name a few. My goal is to help you learn to make simple "Outside of the Box" healthy meals that will free up your time to do more of the things you love. It's time my friends to *Shop, Cook, Eat: Outside of the Box*.

# Sharing my passion for food...

*...with you!*

# hands on

# Why cook?

You owe it to yourself to cook. Cooking at home in your kitchen using fresh, whole ingredients is one of the most important things you can do for your health. Remember; "You are what you eat." So, fuel your body with fresh food prepared in your very own kitchen. Also, consider the following:

• Cooking gives you freedom. You are free from the boxed, processed foods and restaurant fare which can be low in nutrients and high in calories, sodium, and other additives, By cooking meals from scratch you take the guesswork out of reading packaged labels – you know exactly what ingredients are used.

• Preparing meals at home can save you money too, and in the long run -- time. You'll want to set aside time in your schedule to grocery shop, prep, and cook. It's easier than you think – you just have to make a plan and stick to it. Think of grocery shopping as a hunting/gathering adventure and you're out to find the best ingredients at the lowest prices.

• Cooking can be a social event. You can show off your culinary skills by providing a meal for friends, and perhaps enlisting their help prepping the vegetables.   There's nothing like preparing and sharing a good meal with family and friends while chatting and laughing.

Cooking is a creative process so let loose and have fun! Use the recipes in this book as your guide. As you gain confidence, feel free to experiment  – that's how some of the best dishes are created.

Never cooked much? No worries. This book is designed for any beginner in the kitchen and will show you how to shop, prepare, and cook delicious simple meals: Outside of the Box.

## Happy shopping, cooking, and eating!

# SHOP

# Grocery Shopping & Planning

**Think of grocery shopping as as a hunting, gathering experience.**

I'll be honest, shopping, cooking, and eating "Outside of the Box" will require a commitment from you. Once a week set aside time to plan your meals and to grocery shop. Having a plan of action will save you time and ultimately make your days easier.

Don't think of the grocery store as a boring, intimidating place. Rather, think of grocery shopping as a hunting, gathering experience where you get to choose goods to fuel your awesome body.

**Keep these things in mind when you set off on your adventure:**

1. Grocery stores are designed to keep you in the store as long as possible. The essential items (produce and dairy) are located on the extreme corners of the store. So you have to pass by lots of other tempting merchandise even if you're just running in for a head of lettuce.

2. The most expensive products are placed at eye level (except for kid's products, which are placed at their eye level).

## Why a Grocery List?

- It helps you plan for your meals and even your snacks.
- It prevents you from going back to the store for the forgotten ingredient.
- It helps you to eat healthier because you'll be less likely to reach for something on impulse.
- It will save you money. You will not be so tempted to grab stuff that is not on the list.

## Making a Grocery List

- Get to know your store. Make your list based on the layout of the store. For example, put fruits and vegetables at the top of your list if the produce department is the first section of the store.
- Write out your list based on the things that you need to maintain a well-stocked kitchen (Kitchen Essentials page 22).
- Check your fridge, freezer, and pantry and add items to the list that you are low on.
- Think about your daily menus for the upcoming week. Many shoppers make one big shopping trip a week and frequent smaller trips for perishable items.
- Don't buy junk food (or buy as little as possible). Junk food costs a lot of money for about zero nutrition. Opt for fresh, whole food (e.g. as found in nature).
- Stick to your list. Avoid impulse buys. They are almost always bad, and even if it's just a couple dollars, they can add up quickly.

# Shopping Tips

A healthy lifestyle begins in your kitchen. That's why it is important to make smart choices in the grocery store. Here are some basic tips to get you started:

**1 SHOP THE PERIMETER**
The perimeter of the grocery store is where most stores feature healthy foods – fresh fruits and vegetables, fish, meat, dairy.

**2 BUY IN BULK**
You'll save money buying the foods you eat regularly in bulk. Beans, grains, nuts, and spices are great bulk-savers. All foods are not cheaper in bulk, however, so make sure to comparison shop.

**3 BUY SEASONALLY**
Eating fruits and vegetables that are in season not only taste better but also saves you money. Eating seasonally allows you to eat locally grown food too.

**4 SHOP FOR BARGAINS**
Check grocery store ads or look for specials while at the store. Plan your meals based on the sale items. If there is a sale on the items you use regularly (broths, canned beans and tomatoes) – stock up.

**5 TRY THE STORE BRANDS**
Brand names are often no better than generic, and you're paying for all the advertising they do to have a brand name. Give the store brand a try; many times you will not even notice a difference.

**6 DON'T SHOP WHEN YOU'RE HUNGRY**
When you're hungry, you want to buy items not on your list.

# Kitchen Essentials

A well-stocked kitchen gives you options, and lets you be creative without having to run to the store every time you want to cook. I often find that I can look in the fridge and pantry and come up with a recipe based on what I have on hand.

With essentials at the ready you can create delicious, wholesome meals in a pinch.

## Fridge

Butter
Cheese:
  Cottage
  Feta
  Mozzarella
  Parmesan
Dijon mustard

Eggs
Mayonnaise
Milk / Non-dairy milk
Sour cream
Yogurt:
  Cultured coconut milk
  Plain Greek

## Herbs & Spices

Kosher or sea salt
Black pepper
Basil
Cayenne pepper
Ground cinnamon
Ground cumin
Ground mustard

Italian seasoning
Nutmeg
Oregano
Paprika
Red chili flakes
Rosemary
Thyme

## Countertop

Garlic
Lemons
Limes
Onions

# Pantry

**Beans:**
Black
Cannellini
Garbanzo
Red Kidney
Refried
**Broth:**
Chicken
Vegetable
**Dried fruit:**
Apricots
Cherries
Cranberries
Dates
Raisins
**Oats:**
Rolled
Steel Cut
**Oils:**
Canola
Cooking oil spray
Coconut
Extra-virgin olive oil
Sesame
**Natural nut butters:**
Almond
Peanut
**Nuts/Seeds:**
Cashews
Chia/Hemp/Flax seeds
Pumpkin seeds
Raw & Sliced almonds
Sunflower seeds
Walnuts

**Rice:**
Brown
Wild
**Whole Grains:**
Barley
Bulgur
Millet
Quinoa
Wheat berries
**Vinegar:**
Balsamic
Rice
White wine
**Other:**
Baking soda
Baking powder
Coconut flakes, unsweetened
Honey
Pure Vanilla Extract
Soy sauce
Tomatoes
Tomato paste, sauce
Whole wheat flour
Worcestershire sauce

# Basic Kitchen Tools

I absolutely love kitchen gadgets. I have all sorts of fun kitchen stuff though we all know you don't need lots of gadgets to cook. Truthfully, you need only a few basic tools to make your well-stocked kitchen complete.

## Must-haves:

Baking sheets, rimmed
Cast iron skillet
Citrus juicer
Colander
Cutting board
Food processor, mini
Frying pan or sauté pan
Garlic press
Grater
Kitchen shears

Knives
- Bread
- Chef's
- Paring

Ladle
Measuring cups
Measuring spoons
Meat Thermometer
Mixing bowls
Peppermill
Saucepan
Spatula
Stockpot
Whisk

# Kitchen Safety Tips

When preparing food follow these tips:

- Keep the kitchen clean.

- Keep hot foods hot.

- Keep cold foods cold.

- Always wash hands between jobs such as making a salad and handling raw meat, poultry, shellfish, fish, and eggs.

- Use separate cutting boards for raw poultry, fish, meat and another cutting board for other foods.

# Kitchen Tips

**1 GET ORGANIZED**
Read the recipe through before you get started. Set out all ingredients and equipment first.

**2 CHOP & PREP**
Chop extra onions, bell peppers, carrots, etc. and stash in the fridge for busy days.

**3 FREEZE FOR EASE**
Double the recipe when you make homemade stocks and sauces and freeze for later use.

**4 SPICE PIZAZZ**
Using fresh herbs can add flair to your dishes and spices can take your meal from ordinary to extra-ordinary in a pinch.

**5 MIX & MATCH**
Everything doesn't have to be made from scratch. If you're in a hurry -- pick up a store bought rotisserie chicken and make your own side dishes.

**6 SUBSTITUTES**
If you're missing an ingredient for a recipe try a similar one. Or maybe you don't like onions leave them out. Be creative. This is your food.

**7 TASTE, TASTE, TASTE**
How else will you know how the food tastes? Make adjustments to seasonings, add more broth, etc. as you cook.

**8 TIME YOUR MEAL**
Timing is important when cooking. Plan so everything is close to done at the same time.

**9 ZAP!**
Use your microwave. It's an easy way to thaw and reheat stocks and sauces, or melt butter and chocolate. Make sure to use glass microwaveable safe dishes.

**10 HAVE FUN!**
There is joy in the kitchen -- cooking and eating.

# REMEMBER...

This is your food! Use the recipes in this book as your guide. If you are missing an ingredient or want to try something a little "Outside of the Box," go for it! To those of you new to cooking, my only suggestion is to try the recipe the way it's written the first time, but next time feel free to make adjustments based on your taste buds or what you have in stock in your fridge or pantry.

*Common swapable/interchangeable items:*

- Oils (Peanut and Sesame have a distinct taste so use with caution)
- Salt (There are a variety; find the one you like)
- Dairy milk for non-dairy milk
- Grains instead of rice
- Experiment with yogurt (Plain is best for low-sugar content)
- Dried herbs for fresh
- Canned beans for fresh cooked beans

## ENOUGH ALREADY LET'S COOK!

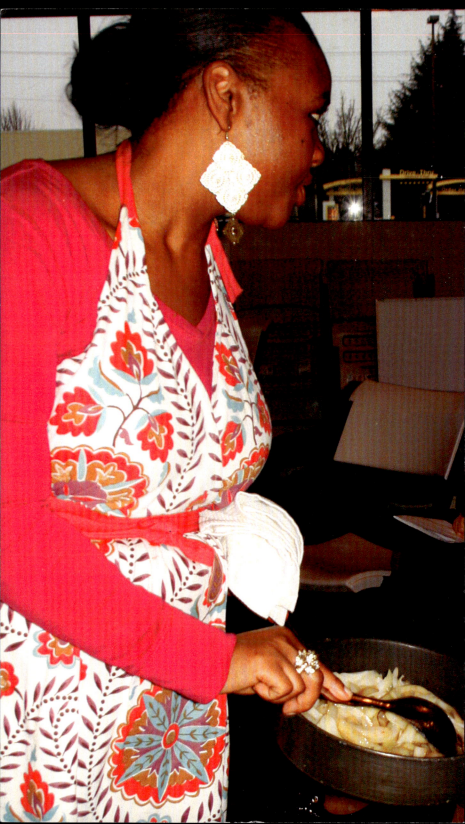

COOK

# BASICS

The basic recipes in this section will make it easy to create a healthy meal quickly. It includes basic cooking tips for grains and beans, for tomato sauce which can be used in lots of dishes, and vegetable stock that will be used time and time again.

BEANS

GRAINS

VEGETABLE STOCK

TOMATO SAUCE

VINAIGRETTES

OLIVE OIL DRIZZLE

HARD-BOILED EGGS

# BASICS: BEANS

Despite their small size, beans offer a big nutritional punch. Beans are loaded with nutrients and are low in fat as well as high in fiber.

Dried beans take a little more time to prepare, but they are lower in sodium and are less expensive than canned beans. Dried beans can be found either pre-packaged or in the bulk section of most grocery stores.

**Follow these directions and use the guide to cook up a pot of beans in a cinch.**

### Preparing Dried Beans:
Place dried beans in a colander, sort through them thoroughly and remove any tiny pebbles or other debris, and then rinse under cold water.

### Soaking Dried Beans:
Large beans need to be soaked before cooking to soften and plump them. There are two methods for soaking beans, the quick-soak method and the long-soak method. Small beans and lentils don't require soaking.

#### Quick-Soak Method:
1. Place dried beans in a large saucepan; add enough water to cover them.
2. Heat to boiling; boil 2 minutes.
3. Remove from heat, cover and let stand for at least 1 hour before cooking. Drain, then cook in fresh cold water.

#### Long-Soak Method:
1. Place dried beans in a large saucepan or bowl; add enough cold water to cover them.
2. Let stand 8 – 12 hours (Soaking longer than 12 hours yields beans with an undesirable mushy consistency.)
3. Drain, then cook in fresh cold water.

**Tip: Beans are a great substitute for meat.**

## How To Cook Dried Beans:

Place soaked beans in a heavy metal pot or saucepan with fresh water or stock. Bring the beans to a boil, and then lower the heat and simmer. Cover and cook until beans are tender. Check chart for cooking times.

Always test a few beans in case they have not cooked evenly. Once the beans are done to your taste, turn the heat off and drain the cooking liquid off. Add a large pinch of kosher salt and several grinds of black pepper.

Cooked beans can be refrigerated for up to four days in your refrigerator or stored in your freezer for up to 6 months.

*Add salt or acidic ingredients; like vinegar, tomatoes or tomato juice, when the beans are just tender. Otherwise, they will slow the cooking process.*

### Large Bean Guide:

| Dried Beans (1 cup dry) | Liquid | Cooking Time |
|---|---|---|
| Anasazi Beans | 4 cups | 1½ hours |
| Black Beans | 3 cups | 1½ - 2 hours |
| Butter Beans | 3 cups | 1½ - 2 hours |
| Cannellini Beans | 3 cups | 1 - 1½ hours |
| Garbanzo Beans (Chickpeas) | 3 cups | 1½ - 2 hours |
| Kidney Beans | 3 cups | 1½ - 2 hours |
| Lima Beans, baby | 3 cups | 1 hour |
| Lima Beans, large | 3 cups | 1 hour |
| Pinto Beans | 3 cups | 1½ - 2 hours |
| Red Beans, small | 3 cups | 1 - 1½ hours |
| Soybeans | 4 cups | 3 - 4 hours |
| White Beans | 4 cups | 1 - 1½ hours |
| White Navy Beans, small | 4 cups | 1½ hours |

### Small Bean Guide:

| Dried Beans (1 cup dry) | Liquid | Cooking Time |
|---|---|---|
| Baby Lentils | 3 - 4 cups | 30 - 45 minutes |
| Green Lentils | 3 - 4 cups | 45 - 60 minutes |
| Red Lentils | 3 - 4 cups | 30 minutes |
| Yellow Lentils | 3 - 4 cups | 30 - 45 minutes |
| Green Split Peas | 3 cups | 45 - 50 minutes |
| Yellow Split Peas | 3 cups | 45 - 50 minutes |
| Black-eyed Peas | 3 cups | 45 - 50 minutes |
| Mung Beans | 3 cups | 1 hour |
| Adzuki Beans | 3 cups | 1 hour |

# BASICS: GRAINS

Whole grains provide a healthy boost of vitamins, minerals, and fiber. Grains make a great addition to meals and are simple to prepare. With a little planning you can have grains on hand for cold grain salads (just toss with chopped vegetables, dressing, and anything else that suits your fancy), or toss a few handfuls into soups.

### Tips for basic grains cooking:

• Plan ahead and cook grains in advance for quick meal preparation. Whole grains will keep in the refrigerator for 3 – 4 days.

• Cook grains in stock to add extra flavor. If you do not have stock, try adding half a carrot, half a stalk of celery, a quarter of an onion and a bay leaf to the cooking water. Or try a crushed clove of garlic and a pinch of red pepper flakes.

### Guide for cooking most grains:

1. Bring cooking liquid to a boil and add grains. Cover with a tight-fitting lid and reduce heat to simmer.
2. Add a half teaspoon of salt halfway through cooking time.
3. Let grains stand for five minutes after cooking to help the grain remain intact.
4. Drain off any remaining liquid.

Grains are done when water is absorbed, they are slightly chewy, and you can fluff them with a fork. See cooking grain guide on next page.

# Grain Guide:

| Grain (1 cup dry) | Liquid | Cooking Time |
|---|---|---|
| Barley, pearl | 2½ cups | 40 minutes |
| Barley, hulled | 3 cups | 45 - 60 minutes |
| Brown Rice | 2½ cups | 50 minutes |
| Bulgur | 2 cups | After boiling, cover and let sit off heat for 10 -15 minutes. |
| Couscous | 1 cup | After boiling, cover and let sit off heat for 5 -10 minutes. |
| Millet | 2 cups | 25 - 30 minutes |
| Oats, regular | 2½ cups | 5 - 10 minutes |
| Oats, steel cut | 4 cups | 30 minutes |
| Polenta | 3 cups | 20 minutes stir often |
| Quinoa | 2 cups | 12 - 15 minutes |
| Spelt berries | 3 cups | 1 hour |
| Wheat berries | 3 cups | 1 hour |

# Grains Galore!

| Start with | Add in any or all | Dress with |
|---|---|---|
| Barley | Dried cranberries, cherries, or raisins<br>Chopped apple<br>Celery<br>Walnuts | Greek yogurt<br>Lemon juice |
| Brown rice | Grated carrots<br>Spinach<br>Cucumber<br>Toasted sunflower seeds | Sunflower oil<br>Rice wine vinegar<br>Ginger<br>Soy sauce |
| Bulgur | Scallions<br>Tomatoes | Olive oil<br>Lemon juice |
| Quinoa | Celery or fennel<br>Orange sections<br>Diced red onion<br>Slivered almonds | Olive oil<br>Mustard<br>White wine vinegar |
| Wheat berries | Apples<br>Cranberries<br>Pecans | Raspberry vinegar<br>Olive oil |

# BASICS: VEGETABLE STOCK

*There's no comparison to the taste of homemade stock. It's simple to make and the ingredients are inexpensive to buy. Best of all, you can make large quantities, freeze it and have it ready for use it in soups, beans, sauces, or for any dish that you want to add more flavor to.*

**PREP TIME:** 5 MINUTES   **TOTAL TIME:** 45 MINUTES   **MAKES:** 8 CUPS

*Ingredients*

4 carrots, unpeeled, quartered
1 large onion, unpeeled, quartered
1 large leek, sliced
2 potatoes, unpeeled, halved
2 celery stalks with leaves, roughly chopped
3 garlic cloves
20 sprigs flat-leaf parsley with stems
Kosher salt
A few black peppercorns

*Directions*

Rinse all of the vegetables.  Then combine all ingredients in a stockpot with 12 cups of water. Simmer gently uncovered for 30 - 40 minutes until the vegetables are tender. Strain the entire contents of the pot through a colander and discard the solids. Let cool before refrigerating or freezing.

Refrigerate for up to 5 days or freeze for up to 6 months.

# BASICS: TOMATO SAUCE

*Tomato sauce is great to have in the fridge and adds zest to vegetables, soups, or any dish.*

**PREP TIME:** 20 MINUTES   **TOTAL TIME:** 45 MINUTES   **MAKES:** 4 CUPS

*Ingredients*

3 tablespoons extra-virgin olive oil
1 large onion, roughly chopped
6 garlic cloves, minced
Kosher salt
Freshly ground black pepper
4 pounds fresh ripe tomatoes, diced
OR
2 (28-ounce) cans diced tomatoes
½ teaspoon Italian seasoning

*Directions*

Heat the olive oil in a large saucepan. Add the onion, sprinkle with ½ teaspoon salt and ¼ teaspoon pepper. Cook until softened 3 - 5 minutes. Then add the tomatoes with their juice and the Italian seasoning. Simmer and stir occasionally until everything comes together and thickens a bit, 20 – 25 minutes. Adjust the seasonings to taste.

This tomato sauce can be refrigerated for 2 weeks or frozen for up to 1 year.

# BASICS: VINAIGRETTES

*Vinaigrettes are simple to make and versatile. They are great for salads, but can be used as a sauce for vegetables, or as a marinade for tofu, chicken, fish, or meat.*

**Don't have a salad dressing shaker bottle?** Place the ingredients in a screw-top jar and shake.

## Lemon

*Ingredients*

¼ cup freshly squeezed lemon juice (2 lemons)
½ cup extra-virgin olive oil
½ teaspoon kosher salt
¼ teaspoon freshly ground black pepper
1 garlic clove, minced

*Directions*

In salad dressing shaker bottle add lemon juice, olive oil, salt, pepper, and garlic. Shake until ingredients are mixed.

## Balsamic

*Ingredients*

½ cup extra-virgin olive oil
¼ cup balsamic vinegar
2 tablespoons Dijon mustard
2 tablespoons freshly squeezed lemon juice
1 teaspoon kosher salt
¼ teaspoon freshly ground black pepper
Dash of Worcestershire sauce
1 garlic clove, minced

*Directions*

In salad dressing shaker bottle add olive oil, balsamic vinegar, Dijon mustard, lemon juice, salt, pepper, Worcestershire sauce, and garlic. Shake until ingredients are mixed.

# BASICS: OLIVE OIL DRIZZLE

*I use this drizzle recipe from Mark Bittman all the time. It's a great, simple sauce to have at the ready. You can use it on cooked vegetables, grains, beans, tofu, meat, poultry, and fish.*

**PREP TIME:** 5 MINUTES   **TOTAL TIME:** 5 MINUTES   **MAKES:** ½ CUP

*Ingredients*

4 tablespoons extra-virgin olive oil
1 tablespoon minced onion, garlic, ginger, shallot, scallion, or lemongrass
2 tablespoons freshly squeezed lemon juice or mild vinegar like balsamic
Kosher salt
Freshly ground black pepper
Water

*Directions*

Put the oil in a small saucepan over medium heat. Add onion, sprinkle with salt and pepper, and cook 1 - 2 minutes, stirring occasionally until it softens. Stir in 2 tablespoons water and the lemon juice; maintain the heat so It bubbles gently for a few seconds but doesn't boil away. Taste, adjust the seasoning, and serve.

# BASICS: HARD-BOILED EGGS

*Here's a foolproof, reliable way to cook boiled eggs. A great addition to salads or eat them straight.*

**PREP TIME:** 5 MINUTES   **TOTAL TIME:** 15 MINUTES   **SERVES:** 2 - 4

*Ingredients*

2 – 4 eggs

*Directions*

Place eggs in a saucepan with enough water to cover them by 1 inch. Bring the water to a boil and remove from the heat. Cover and let stand for 12 minutes. Drain and rinse under cold running water.

Unpeeled hard-boiled eggs can be stored in the refrigerator for up to one week.

# SNACKS

SPICY ROASTED CHICKPEAS

KALE CHIPS

BAKED TORTILLA CHIPS

BROWN BAG POPCORN

FRESH VEGETABLE KEBABS

FRUIT KEBABS

CASHEW ENERGY BAR

CHOCOLATE COCONUT ENERGY BAR

# SPICY ROASTED CHICKPEAS

*A fun, spicy, pop-in-your-mouth snack – and a great source of protein.*

**PREP TIME:** 5 MINUTES   **TOTAL TIME:** 30 MINUTES   **SERVES:** 6 - 8

*Ingredients*

¼ cup extra-virgin olive oil
2 cups garbanzo beans (chickpeas), rinsed and drained
¼ teaspoon cayenne pepper
1 teaspoon ground cumin
Sprinkle of kosher salt
Grated zest of half of a lime

*Directions*

Preheat oven to 450 degrees.

Pour the well-drained chickpeas onto a rimmed baking sheet, and roast for 10 minutes. Meanwhile, in a medium bowl, combine olive oil, cayenne pepper, ground cumin, salt, and lime zest. Toss chickpeas into mixture in bowl and combine. Return chickpea mixture to baking sheet and roast 10 – 15 minutes. Let cool for 1 – 2 minutes. Serve warm.

# KALE CHIPS

*Kale chips rule!*

**PREP TIME:** 5 MINUTES   **TOTAL TIME:** 30 MINUTES   **SERVES:** 2 - 4

*Ingredients*

1 bunch kale
1 tablespoon olive oil
Kosher salt to taste

*Directions*

Preheat oven to 350 degrees. With a knife or kitchen shears carefully remove the leaves from the thick stems and tear into bite size pieces. Wash and thoroughly dry kale with a salad spinner or use a clean dry dishtowel. Lay on a baking sheet and toss with the olive oil and salt. Bake until the edges brown but are not burnt, 20 - 25 minutes.

# BAKED TORTILLA CHIPS

*Who needs store-bought tortilla chips? You can make your own warm, crispy baked chips fresh from your oven.*

**PREP TIME:** 5 MINUTES   **TOTAL TIME:** 20 MINUTES   **SERVES:** 2 -4

*Ingredients*

12 (6 inch) corn tortillas
1 tablespoon canola oil
Kosher salt

*Directions*

Preheat the oven to 350 degrees. Brush both sides of the tortillas with the oil. Stack the tortillas and cut the pile into sixths to make chips. Spread the chips out in a single layer on rimmed baking sheet and season with salt. Bake until golden brown and crisp, After 12-15 minutes, turn chips over once. Serve.

**Serve with:**
Chili (page 107)
Guacamole (page 111)
Fresh Salsa (page 113 )

# BROWN BAG POPCORN

*When I first discovered this technique I was floored, You can make your own microwave popcorn without all the additives. Try it. You can melt a little butter and drizzle it on it if you like. I do!*

**PREP TIME:** LESS THAN 5 MINUTES   **TOTAL TIME:** 5 MINUTES   **SERVES:** 3

*Ingredients*

½ cup unpopped popcorn
1 teaspoon canola oil
½ teaspoon salt, or to taste
Butter, optional

*Directions*

In a small bowl, mix together the unpopped popcorn, oil, and salt. Pour the coated corn into a paper bag. Fold the top of the bag over twice to seal in the ingredients. Cook in the microwave at full power for 2½ - 3 minutes, or until you hear pauses of about 2 seconds between pops. Carefully open the bag to avoid burning yourself, and pour into a serving bowl. Melt butter in microwave if using. Grub!

# FRESH VEGETABLE KEBABS

*The tangy vinaigrette brings out the natural sweetness in the fresh vegetables.*

**PREP TIME:** 10 MINUTES    **TOTAL TIME:** 1 HR, 10 MIN    **SERVES:** 2

*Ingredients*

8 cherry tomatoes
1 large zucchini, cut crosswise into ¾-inch thick slices
1 large yellow bell pepper, seeded and cut into 1½ inch wedges
1 tablespoon olive oil
2 garlic cloves, finely minced
1 tablespoon balsamic vinegar
Freshly ground black pepper to taste

*Directions*

Mix the tomatoes, zucchini, bell pepper and garlic in a resealable plastic bag. Drizzle the vegetables with the oil and vinegar, and then sprinkle evenly with pepper. Close bag and shake to mix. Allow the vegetables to marinate for 1 hour at room temperature. Place the vegetables on 2 skewers. Serve.

# FRUIT KEBABS

*Let your taste buds guide your choice of fresh, in season produce. This is a fun way to eat fruit.*

**PREP TIME:** 10 MINUTES   **TOTAL TIME:** 10 MINUTES   **SERVES:** 4

*Ingredients*

### Fruit Kebab #1

¾ cup fresh pineapple, cut into 1½ inch cubes
¾ cup cantaloupe, cut into 1½ inch cubes
1 banana, thick sliced
6 whole strawberries, cored

### Fruit Kebab #2

1 firm, ripe peach, pitted, and cut into 8 wedges
2 firm, ripe plums, pitted, and cut in half
1 firm, ripe apricot, pitted, and cut into 4 wedges
6 whole strawberries, cored

*Directions*

Alternately place the fruit on skewers. Serve.

**No skewers? Put the fruit in a bowl and drizzle with freshly squeezed lime juice.**

# CASHEW ENERGY BARS

*A whole food energy boost. Simple ingredients and easy to make. You'll be whipping these up all the time.*

**PREP TIME:** 5 MINUTES   **TOTAL TIME:** 10 MINUTES   **MAKES:** 4 - 6 BARS

*Ingredients*

2 cup dates, pitted and roughly chopped
2 cups cashews
Pinch of kosher salt, optional

*Directions*

Process dates in food processor until finely chopped. Place in a medium bowl. Process cashews in food processor until finely chopped, then add to processed dates. Add salt, if using. Mix together with your hands until thoroughly combined. Use your hands to shape into bars (If mixture is too crumbly, try applying more pressure, if still too crumbly, add more processed dates). If you have leftover cashew crumbs feel free to roll your bars in the crumbs. Store in airtight containers or freeze in zipper-locked plastic bags.

# CHOCOLATE COCONUT ENERGY BARS

**PREP TIME:** 5 MINUTES   **TOTAL TIME:** 10 MINUTES   **MAKES:** 4 - 6 BARS

*Ingredients*

2 cups dates, pitted and roughly chopped
2 cups walnuts, chopped
3 teaspoons cocoa powder
½ cup unsweetened shredded coconut flakes
1 teaspoon vanilla extract

*Directions*

Place chopped dates in food processor and process until finely chopped. Place in a medium bowl. Place walnuts in food processor. Pulse a few times until pieces are fairly small, then add processes dates, cocoa powder and vanilla and process until thoroughly combined. Add coconut flakes and pulse a few times. Use your hands to shape into bars. Store in airtight containers or freeze in zipper-locked plastic bags.

# MAKE IT FAST

SANTA FE CHICKEN WRAPS

GREEK WRAPS

VEGGIE WRAPS

LETTUCE WRAPS

VEGETABLE FRIED RICE BOWL

MEXICAN RICE BOWL

GREEK QUINOA BOWL

ZUCCHINI & MUSHROOM TACOS

# SANTA FE CHICKEN WRAPS

*Using a store-bought rotisserie chicken makes this spicy and cool wrap a cinch.*

**PREP TIME:** 10 MINUTES   **TOTAL TIME:** 20 MINUTES   **SERVES:** 4

*Ingredients*

### For the Santa Fe Chicken Salad
⅔ cup sour cream
3 tablespoons freshly squeezed lime juice (1 lime)
½ teaspoon kosher salt
¼ teaspoon freshly ground black pepper
¼ teaspoon chili powder
¼ teaspoon cumin
2 – 3 green onions, sliced
2 cups chicken, shredded
⅔ cup black beans, drained
⅓ cup red bell pepper, diced

*Directions*

### For the Santa Fe Chicken Salad:
In a medium bowl, combine the sour cream, lime juice, salt, pepper, chili powder, and cumin. Stir to combine.

Add the chicken and green onion to the sour cream mixture. Stir until the chicken is well coated. Fold in the black beans and bell pepper. Cover and chill until ready to serve.

### For the Wraps
Santa Fe Chicken Salad
4 (8 inch) tortillas, warmed
Salad greens or baby spinach
Avocado slices
Fresh Salsa (page 113)

### To warm tortillas:
Place tortillas in single stack. Wrap damp paper towels around the tortillas to keep them moist while heating. Heat in microwave for 30 seconds.

### Wrapping it up:
To make wraps, evenly divide Santa Fe Chicken salad, salad greens or baby spinach, and avocado slices between the tortillas. Fold up the ends and roll the wrap to seal it. Slice in half. Serve with Fresh Salsa (page 113) on the side, if desired.

# GREEK WRAPS

*Greek cuisine all wrapped up.*

**PREP TIME:** 20 MINUTES   **TOTAL TIME:** 20 MINUTES   **SERVES:** 4

*Ingredients*

2 cups rotisserie deli chicken, shredded
1 cup cherry or grape tomatoes, halved
¼ cup red onion, diced
¼ cup cucumber, diced
12 Kalamata or black olives, halved
2 - 3 tablespoons Lemon Vinaigrette (page 39)
1 cup baby spinach leaves, chopped
4 (8 inch) tortillas, warmed
¼ cup feta cheese, crumbled

*Directions*

Place chicken tomatoes, onion, cucumber, olives and vinaigrette in small bowl. Toss together.

## To warm tortillas:
Place tortillas in single stack. Wrap damp paper towels around the tortillas to keep them moist while heating. Heat in microwave for 30 seconds.

## Wrapping it up:
Divide and spread baby spinach over tortillas. Top each with equal amounts of chicken mixture. Fold up the ends and roll the wrap to seal it. Slice in half.

*To make this a meatless wrap, simply omit the chicken. Double the quantity of the other ingredients (except Vinaigrette) to fill it out.*

# VEGGIE WRAPS

*Quinoa and beans provide a protein boost to this meatless wrap.
It's a veggie delight!*

**PREP TIME:** 10 MINUTES   **TOTAL TIME:** 20 MINUTES   **SERVES:** 4

*Ingredients*

3 – 4 cups baby spinach leaves, chopped
2 cups quinoa, cooked
1 cup cannellini beans, cooked or use your choice of beans
1 red bell pepper, sliced
¼ cup red onion, sliced
4 (8 inch) tortillas, warmed
Balsamic or Lemon Vinaigrette (page 39)

*Directions*

## To warm tortillas:
Place tortillas in single stack. Wrap damp paper towels around the
tortillas to keep them moist while heating. Heat in microwave for
30 seconds.

## Wrapping it up:
Divide and spread ingredients evenly among the tortillas. Fold up
the ends and roll the wrap to seal it. Slice in half. Eat up!

# LETTUCE WRAPS

*My twist on the popular P.F. Chang's lettuce wraps. Tasty and fresh.*

**PREP TIME:** 10 MINUTES   **TOTAL TIME:** 25 MINUTES   **SERVES:** 4

*Ingredients*

12 large iceberg lettuce leaves

## Toppings
1 cucumber, diced
¼ cup carrots, shredded
½ cup cilantro, chopped
½ cup almonds or peanuts, roughly chopped
Crispy chow mein noodles, optional

## Teriyaki sauce:
2 tablespoons soy sauce
1 tablespoon rice vinegar
½ cup honey
1 garlic clove, minced
1 teaspoon fresh ginger, grated and peeled

## Filling
5 teaspoons sesame oil
1 pound skinless, boneless chicken breasts, diced
1 garlic clove, finely minced
1 cup cremini mushrooms, diced
2 teaspoons kosher salt
¼ teaspoon white pepper
3 tablespoons of Teriyaki sauce (recipe above)

*To make this a meatless wrap, simply omit the chicken. Double the quantity of the other ingredients to fill it out.*

*Directions*

**For toppings:** Chop and dice toppings and set aside.

**For Teriyaki sauce:** In a small bowl, combine soy sauce, vinegar, honey, garlic, and ginger. Set aside.

**For filling:** Add 3 teaspoons of oil to large frying pan. Heat oil over high heat until it glistens about 1 minute. Meanwhile, season chicken with salt, and white pepper. Add chicken to pan and cook until mostly cooked through, about 5 minutes. Remove.

Turn the heat down to medium-high, add 2 teaspoons of oil. Wait 1 minute; add garlic and mushrooms. Cook about 3 minutes and then add chicken back. Stir fry all ingredients for 2 more minutes and drizzle with sauce. Set aside to cool.

Place filling in lettuce leaves, add toppings and drizzle with teriyaki sauce. Grab a napkin, these can get messy!

# VEGETABLE FRIED RICE BOWL

*This veggie studded rice is great as an entrée. The key to good fried rice is starting with cold cooked rice.*

**PREP TIME:** 20 MINUTES  **TOTAL TIME:** 30 MINUTES  **SERVES** 4

*Ingredients*

3 - 4 cups cooked brown rice
2 cups small broccoli florets
3 tablespoons peanut or vegetable oil
1 bunch scallions, chopped
¼ head cabbage, chopped
1 red bell pepper, cored, seeded, and chopped
2 tablespoons garlic, minced
2 eggs, lightly beaten, optional
2 tablespoons soy sauce
Kosher salt to taste
Sesame seeds, optional

*When it comes to vegetables, don't fre Look at what you've got in the crisper first. Improvise. Just make sure to have all vegetables ready to go. The work in thi dish is in prepping th vegetables.*

*Directions*

Steam broccoli, 2 minutes or until crisp-tender. Drain; cool. Heat a wok or frying pan and add 1 tablespoon of oil. When the oil is hot, add the eggs. Cook, stirring, until they are lightly scrambled but not too dry. Remove the eggs and clean out the pan.

Add 1 tablespoon oil, add ¾ of the chopped scallions and bell pepper and cook, stirring occasionally, until they soften and begin to brown, about 3 minutes. Lower the heat if the mixture starts to brown too quickly. Transfer the vegetables to a bowl.

Add the cabbage to the same pan with a little more oil and cook, over high heat, stirring occasionally, until nicely browned about 5 minutes. Add to the bowl with the vegetables.

Put the remaining oil in the skillet, followed by the garlic. Begin to add the rice, a little at a time, using a wooden spoon to break up the clumps. Cook until the rice is crispy, about 5 minutes. Return the vegetables to the pan and fold everything until combined. Add soy sauce and salt and to taste.

**For bowls:** Serve in individual bowls. Top with remaining chopped scallions and sesame seeds, if using.

**Other grains to try:** Instead of the rice, use cooked quinoa, or large-kernel grains like wheat berries or barley. Just make sure they're relatively dry before starting.

**Other ingredients to try:** Peeled shrimp, cooked bacon pork, or chicken.

# MEXICAN RICE BOWL

*Inspired by Chipotle's burrito in a bowl, but better. Simple, fresh and delicious.*

**PREP TIME:** 5 MINUTES   **TOTAL TIME:** 30 MINUTES   **SERVES:** 4

*Ingredients*

## For Cilantro Rice

2 cups white rice, cooked
1 teaspoon extra-virgin olive oil
Freshly squeezed lime juice (2 limes)
A handful of cilantro, chopped
Kosher salt to taste

## For Toppings

2 cups rotisserie deli chicken, shredded
2 cups black beans, cooked, drained
3 tomatoes, diced
1 red onion, diced
Avocado slices
Fresh Salsa (page 113)
Lime wedges for drizzling, optional

*Directions*

**For Cilantro Rice:** Bring the rice,and water to a boil in a saucepan over high heat. Reduce heat to medium-low, cover, and simmer until the rice is tender, 20 to 25 minutes. Remove from the heat, add the lime juice, olive oil, cilantro, and salt; fluff with a fork.

**For bowls:** Divide the cilantro rice evenly among 4 individual serving bowls. Top with black beans, tomatoes, onion, and avocado slices. Squeeze fresh lime juice over ingredients. Serve.

**Instead of rice, use quinoa.**

# GREEK QUINOA BOWL

*Greek goodness in a bowl.*

**PREP TIME:** 5 MINUTES    **TOTAL TIME:** 25 MINUTES    **SERVES:** 4

*Ingredients*

2 cups quinoa, cooked
½ cup Kalamata olives, halved
1 red onion, diced
1 cup cherry or grape tomatoes, halved
½ cup artichoke hearts, chopped
½ cup feta cheese, crumbled
Kosher salt to taste
Freshly ground pepper to taste
Lemon Vinaigrette (page 39)

*Directions*

In a large bowl, gently toss all ingredients together. Add salt and pepper to taste.

**For bowls:** Divide evenly among individual bowls. Drizzle with lemon vinaigrette. Dig in!

# ZUCCHINI & MUSHROOM TACOS

*Try this meatless version of a Mexican favorite.*

**PREP TIME:** 20 MINUTES   **TOTAL TIME:** 20 MINUTES   **SERVES:** 4

*Ingredients*

3 tablespoons extra-virgin olive oil
3 medium zucchini, cut into ½-inch-wide slices on the diagonal
1 pound cremini mushrooms, stemmed
1 ½ bunches scallions, root ends trimmed
Kosher salt to taste
Freshly ground black pepper to taste
8 (6-inch) white corn tortillas
½ cup feta cheese, crumbled
1 lime, cut into wedges, for serving
Fresh Salsa (page 113), for serving

*Directions*

**For filling:** Heat a tablespoon of oil in a large sauté pan on medium high heat. Season vegetables with salt and pepper. Sauté vegetables separately; 6 minutes for mushrooms and 8 minutes for zucchini. Set aside.

**For tortillas:** Add enough oil to lightly cover the bottom of a large skillet. Heat skillet to medium high. Add a tortilla to the pan. Move it around a bit, and turn it over so that it spreads around the oil. Let the tortilla heat until it develops little bubbles of air pockets on both sides. Repeat with each tortilla.

**For tacos:** Place 1 tortilla on each serving plate; cover evenly with mushrooms and zucchini. Using kitchen shears, snip scallions over vegetables. Top with fresh salsa, and sprinkle with feta. Serve with lime wedges.

# BREAKFAST

BLUEBERRY BANANA KALE SMOOTHIE

GO GREEN DRINK

OPEN-FACED EGG TOMATO SANDWICH

CLASSIC OMELETTE

FRUIT SEED WHEATBERRY BOWL

GRANOLA FRUIT NUT CRUNCH

STEEL CUT OATMEAL

# BLUEBERRY BANANA KALE SMOOTHIE

Smoothies are a great instant breakfast or anytime treat. You can use fresh or frozen fruit. Switch up the fruit, yogurt -- the possibilities are up to you. This one is packed with nutrients and flavor.

**PREP TIME:** 5 MINUTES   **TOTAL TIME:** 5 MINUTES   **SERVES:** 2

*Ingredients*

1 ripe medium banana
½ cup blueberries
Handful of kale leaves
½ cup non-fat plain yogurt
½ cup orange juice or juice of your choice, optional
2 teaspoons chia, flax, or hemp seeds, optional
1 cup ice

*Directions*

Combine ingredients in a blender and blend until smooth.

# GO GREEN DRINK

My friend Katina Benenate was looking for ways to sneak more greens into her diet. This is her low-fat, high-fiber breakfast (or anytime) drink.

**PREP TIME:** 5 MINUTES  **TOTAL TIME:** 5 MINUTES  **SERVES:** 2

*Ingredients*

1 cup kale
1 cup spinach
1 cup swiss chard
1 ripe medium banana
½ lime, juiced
½ cup strawberries (or berry of your choice)
2 teaspoons chia, flax, or hemp seeds, optional
1 cup ice

*Directions*

Combine ingredients in a blender and blend until smooth.

# OPEN-FACED EGG TOMATO SANDWICH

*I favor savory breakfasts. This sandwich fits the bill.*

**PREP TIME:** 5 MINUTES   **TOTAL TIME:** 35 MINUTES   **SERVES:** 2

*Ingredients*

Roasted Plum Tomatoes (page 82)
2 slices of 100% whole grain bread
2 tablespoons butter
4 large eggs
Pinch of kosher salt
Crack of freshly ground black pepper

*Directions*

Prepare roasted plum tomatoes.

Toast bread in toaster. Spread each slice with a tablespoon of butter. Set aside.

Scramble eggs in bowl add salt and pepper to taste. Spray cooking spray in skillet. Heat skillet on medium heat. Pour the eggs in skillet. Don't scramble the eggs instead allow them to lay flat almost like an omelette. Once they are set fold and remove.

Assemble sandwich: Toast, eggs, and tomatoes on top.

# CLASSIC OMELETTE

*A simple, inexpensive meal with unlimited options. Great for dinner too – think "Outside of the Box."*

**PREP TIME:** 5 MINUTES   **TOTAL TIME:** 10 MINUTES   **SERVES:** 1

*Ingredients*

2 eggs
¼ to ⅓ cup of filling
1 teaspoon butter or cooking spray
1 tablespoon milk or water
Kosher salt to taste
Freshly ground black pepper to taste

**If time allows, bring egg to room temperature -- they'll whip up nicely and the omelette will be fluffier. Or, for an even fluffier omelette, add a teaspoon of crème of tartar.**

*Directions*

First, prepare one of the fillings on the next page. A basic rule of thumb is that you need one quarter to one third cup of filling for every two eggs. If you are making a cheese omelette, shred or finely grate your choice of cheese and set aside.

Break the eggs into a small bowl, and add the water or milk, herbs (if recipe calls for them), salt and pepper and whisk with a fork.

Preheat an 8-inch nonstick skillet over medium heat and swirl the butter or cooking spray in the pan. Pour in the egg mixture and swirl it in the pan. For a few seconds, gently stir the egg mixture with a heat resistant rubber spatula (as if you were going to make scrambled eggs) and then swirl the eggs in the pan to make a nice round appearance. Reduce the heat to avoid any scorching. Continue cooking for about 1 minute. The eggs will be set on the bottom, but be slightly liquid on top.

Flip the omelette, and remove it from the heat. Add cheese (if recipe calls for it) over the center of the omelette and top it off with the remaining ingredients (if recipe calls for).
Serve immediately.

**It is important to use a non-stick skillet, so that the omelet does not stick to the bottom or the side. The pan should be really clean, or the eggs could stick. If using a non-stick pan – you can leave out the butter for a much more calorie-conscious meal!**

70

## Vegetable:

In a small skillet, sauté one tablespoon of butter before adding
3 tablespoons red and green bell pepper, chopped
2 tablespoons tomato, chopped
2 tablespoons zucchini, chopped
2 tablespoons mushrooms, chopped
Sauté until tender.

## Southwestern:
1 tablespoon Monterey Jack cheese, grated
2 tablespoons Fresh Salsa (page 113)

## Cheese:
3 tablespoons finely grated swiss, parmesan, or cheddar cheese

## Herb:
½ teaspoon fresh Italian parsley, medium chopped
½ teaspoon fresh basil, medium chopped
½ teaspoon fresh chives, thin sliced
½ teaspoon fresh tarragon, thin sliced

**Substitute dried herbs --(dried herbs have a stronger flavor so use one-third less)**

# FRUIT SEED WHEAT BERRY BOWL

*A delightful way to get the morning started. This is one of my favorite breakfasts sometimes I eat it for a snack in between meals too. The wheatberries and seeds provide a good crunch against the creamy texture of the yogurt and the fruit adds a hint of sweetness. It's like heaven in a bowl and best of all, it's nutrient dense.*

**PREP TIME:** 5 MINUTES   **TOTAL TIME:** 5 MINUTES   **SERVES:** 1

*Ingredients*

½ - 1 cup wheat berries, cooked
½ - 1 cup cultured coconut milk "yogurt"
1 apple, diced
A handful each dried cranberries and diced dried apricots
A generous sprinkle of pumpkin seeds and sunflower seeds
1 teaspoon chia, flax, or hemp seeds

*Directions*

Scoop the wheat berries into an individual bowl, top with yogurt, apple, dried cranberries and apricots, pumpkin, sunflower, and chia seeds. Grub.

**There are no rules here – start with cooked wheatberries, yogurt to bind, and add any fruit, seeds, or nuts you like.**

# GRANOLA FRUIT NUT CRUNCH

*This granola recipe is great for breakfast; just top it with your favorite plain yogurt. It is also great as a snack. You can use different nuts, seeds, and dried fruits to create something new each time. Think "Outside of the Box."*

**PREP TIME:** 5 MINUTES  **TOTAL TIME:** 25 MINUTES  **SERVES:** 6

*Ingredients*

2 cups old fashioned or quick-cooking (not instant) oatmeal
1 cup unsweetened shredded coconut
½ cup whole or sliced almonds
6 tablespoons vegetable oil
3 tablespoons honey
½ cup dried cranberries
¼ cup dried apricots, diced

*Directions*

Preheat oven to 350 degrees.

In a large bowl, toss the oatmeal, coconut, almonds, oil, and honey until combined. Pour onto a rimmed baking sheet and bake, stirring occasionally with a wooden spoon, until golden brown and crunchy, about 20 minutes. Remove from oven. Let cool on sheet pan. Once cool add dried cranberries and apricots. Serve immediately or the granola can be kept in an airtight container in the refrigerator for up to one week.

# STEEL CUT OATMEAL

*I love a warm filling bowl of oats to start my day. Try steel cut oats; they give you the best bang for your nutrient buck. Keep in mind they take a little longer to cook so you may want to cook them ahead of time and refrigerate until ready to serve.*

**PREP TIME:** 5 MINUTES  **TOTAL TIME:** 30 MINUTES  **SERVES:** 4

*Ingredients*

3 cups water
1 cup steel cut oats
¼ teaspoon salt
Maple syrup, milk or non-dairy milk, or butter, any combination to taste

*Directions*

Bring water and salt to a boil. Add oats, reduce heat, cover, and cook 20 - 25 minutes (depending on how chewy you like your cereal). Stir occasionally. Remove from heat and let stand a few minutes before serving.

## Add-ins

2 tablespoons dried cherries,1 tablespoon chopped almonds
¼ cup blueberries, 1 tablespoon chopped walnuts, dash of cinnamon
¼ cup diced apple, 2 tablespoons dried cranberries

# FARMER'S MARKET

BAKED SWEET POTATO FRIES

BAKED SWEET POTATOES

ROASTED PLUM TOMATOES

PARMESAN ROASTED CAULIFLOWER

ROASTED PEPPERS

GARLIC ROASTED ASPARAGUS

ROASTED BRUSSELS SPROUTS

SAUTÉED COLLARD GREENS

# BAKED SWEET POTATO FRIES

*Naturally sweet with a touch of salt. Warning: These fries are highly addictive.*

**PREP TIME:** 5 MINUTES   **TOTAL TIME:** 35 MINUTES   **SERVES:** 4

Ingredients

1 ½ pounds sweet potatoes, peeled (2 medium potatoes)
1 tablespoon canola oil
½ teaspoon kosher salt, plus more to taste
Cooking spray

Directions

Preheat the oven to 450 degrees.

Cut the potatoes lengthwise into ¼-inch thick matchsticks. Place in a plastic sealable bag, add the oil and ½ teaspoon salt. Shake until well coated. Spray a rimmed baking sheet with cooking spray. Arrange the potatoes in a single layer on the baking sheet and bake until tender and crisp, about 30 minutes. Season with additional salt, to taste. Serve immediately.

# BAKED SWEET POTATOES

*No toppings needed. Just bake and enjoy!*

**PREP TIME:** 5 MINUTES   **TOTAL TIME:** 1 HR, 5 MINUTES   **SERVES:** 2 - 4

*Ingredients*

2 - 4 medium sweet potatoes, unpeeled

*Directions*

Preheat oven to 400 degrees.

Pierce each sweet potato several times with a fork. Place the sweet potatoes on a rimmed baking sheet lined with foil. Bake until tender, about one hour. Allow to cool slightly. Serve.

> *Craving something Outside of the Box? Try topping the potatoes with maple syrup, cinnamon, pecans, or orange zest.*

# ROASTED PLUM TOMATOES

*I never met a tomato I didn't like. I especially like roasting them. They can add flavor and texture to any dish. Try them atop an open faced breakfast sandwich (page 82) or eat them straight.*

**PREP TIME:** 5 MINUTES   **TOTAL TIME:** 35 MINUTES   **SERVES:** 4

*Ingredients*

8 plum tomatoes, halved lengthwise
1 tablespoon extra-virgin olive oil
¼ teaspoon dried thyme
1 teaspoon kosher salt
Freshly ground black pepper to taste

*Directions*

Preheat oven to 425 degrees.

Place tomatoes on a rimmed baking sheet; sprinkle with remaining ingredients until coated. Arrange in a single layer, cut sides up. Bake until soft with golden brown edges, about 30 minutes. Serve immediately.

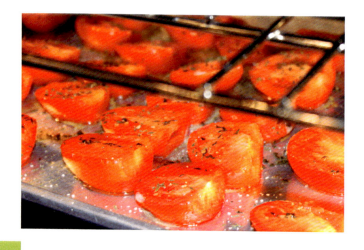

# PARMESAN ROASTED CAULIFLOWER

*Until I found this Roasted Cauliflower with parmesan cheese recipe from Barefoot Contessa, I never really cared much for cauliflower. This recipe is a winner.*

**PREP TIME:** 5 MINUTES    **TOTAL TIME:** 45 MINUTES    **SERVES:** 6

*Ingredients*

1 large head of cauliflower
3 tablespoons extra-virgin olive oil
Kosher salt to taste
Freshly ground black pepper to taste
1 cup parmesan cheese, grated

*Directions*

Preheat oven to 400 degrees.

Remove the outer green leaves from the cauliflower and cut into florets. In two cast iron skillets or on a rimmed baking sheet, toss cauliflower with olive oil, and season generously with salt and pepper. Roast until cauliflower is browned and tender, 35 - 40 minutes. Toss cauliflower about halfway through. Sprinkle with parmesan cheese and bake 1 - 2 minutes more. Serve hot or warm.

# ROASTED PEPPERS

*Insanely delicious. Roasting intensifies the sweetness of the peppers.*

**PREP TIME:** 5 MINUTES   **TOTAL TIME:** 50 MINUTES   **SERVES:** 4

*Ingredients*

4 (red, yellow, or orange) peppers
2 tablespoons extra-virgin olive oil
Kosher salt to taste
Freshly ground black pepper to taste

*Directions*

Preheat oven to 450 degrees. Wash and dry peppers. Place peppers on aluminum foil-lined rimmed baking sheet. Drizzle with olive oil. Sprinkle with salt and pepper. Roast until the skins are completely wrinkled and the peppers are charred, 35 - 40 minutes.

Set aside for 30 minutes or until the peppers are cool enough to handle. Remove the stem from each pepper and cut them in quarters. Remove the peels and seeds and place the peppers in a bowl along with any juices that have collected. Discard the stems, peels, and seeds. Serve or cover with plastic wrap and refrigerate for up to a week.

---

*Look at all the ways you can use roasted peppers:*

*By themselves*
*On a green salad*
*In a wrap or on a sandwich*
*Tossed with grains or pasta*
*Puréed in a blender or food processor with 1 cup cream cheese, sour cream, or garbanzo beans to make a spread*

# GARLIC ROASTED ASPARAGUS

*I'm a fan of simple food. This recipe combines simple ingredients and is bursting with flavor thanks to the fresh squeezed lemon juice.*

**PREP TIME:** 5 MINUTES   **TOTAL TIME:** 25 MINUTES   **SERVES:** 4

*Ingredients*

2 pounds asparagus, trimmed and rinsed
3 tablespoons extra-virgin olive oil
2 garlic cloves, finely minced
Kosher salt to taste
Freshly ground black pepper to taste
A good squeeze of fresh lemon juice

*Directions*

Preheat the oven to 425 degrees.

> The easiest way to remove the tough ends is to flex the asparagus until it snaps and discard the thick end.

Place the asparagus on a rimmed baking sheet. Toss the asparagus with the olive oil, garlic, salt, and pepper. Bake until the asparagus is tender and tips are lightly browned, 15 - 20 minutes. (The cooking time will depend on thickness of the stalks). Remove from the oven and drizzle with lemon juice. Adjust the seasoning to taste.

# ROASTED BRUSSELS SPROUTS

*I think roasting is by far the best method for cooking brussels sprouts. Roasting really brings out the sweetness (reminiscent of cabbage) and crisps the outer leaves. I'm weak for the crispy outer leaves.*

**PREP TIME:** 5 MINUTES   **TOTAL TIME:** 50 MINUTES   **SERVES:** 4

*Ingredients*

1½  pounds brussels sprouts
3 tablespoons extra-virgin olive oil
2 teaspoons kosher salt
1 teaspoon freshly ground black pepper

*Directions*

Preheat oven to 425 degrees.

Trim the stem ends of the brussels sprouts and pull off any yellow outer leaves.

On a rimmed baking sheet or two cast iron skillets toss with olive oil, salt and pepper. Place in oven. Stir once halfway through. Cook until crisp, and golden brown outside, and tender inside, about 40-45 minutes.

*In a hurry? Cut brussels sprouts in half and reduce cook time to 25-35 minutes.*

# SAUTÉED COLLARD GREENS

*A heart healthy version of a southern classic. Tasty!*

**PREP TIME:** 5 MINUTES   **TOTAL TIME:** 25 MINUTES   **SERVES:** 6

*Ingredients*

2 bunches of collard greens
3 tablespoons extra-virgin olive oil
2 garlic cloves, sliced
1 teaspoon kosher salt
½ teaspoon freshly ground black pepper
⅛ teaspoon red pepper flakes
1 tablespoon vinegar

*Directions*

In a large skillet, heat the olive oil. Add the garlic and sauté over medium heat for about 1 minute.  Be careful not to let the garlic brown. Remove garlic. Set aside, Add the greens in 3 batches, allowing each batch to wilt before adding the next. Add salt and pepper toss it all together and cook for 15-20 minutes. Sprinkle with red pepper flakes, add cooked garlic, and drizzle with vinegar. Serve straight away.

# SOUP & SALAD

SWEET POTATO BISQUE

SIMPLY UNFORGETTABLE TOMATO SOUP

LENTIL SOUP

COOL FRUIT SOUP

AVOCADO TOMATO SALAD

WHEATBERRY SPINACH SALAD

GREEK SALAD

CAPRESE SALAD

GREEN BEAN & POTATO SALAD

ANY SEASON FRUIT SALAD

# SWEET POTATO BISQUE

*Naturally sweet and oh so creamy!*

**PREP TIME:** 5 MINUTES   **TOTAL TIME:** 30 MINUTES   **SERVES:** 4

*Ingredients*

1 tablespoon butter
1 onion, chopped
3 cups (½-inch) chunks sweet potatoes, peeled
2 cups vegetable stock (page 36)
1 teaspoon dried thyme
⅛ teaspoon cayenne pepper
1 cup milk
Kosher salt to taste
Freshly ground black pepper to taste

*Directions*

In large pot, melt butter and cook onion until tender, about 4 minutes.

Add sweet potatoes and stock. Bring to a boil. Cover, reduce the heat and simmer for 15 minutes or until potatoes are tender. Pour mixture into food processor and blend until smooth; return to pot. Add thyme, cayenne and milk. Cook over low heat just until heated through. Season to taste. Serve immediately.

# SIMPLY UNFORGETTABLE TOMATO SOUP

*I served this tomato soup at New Seasons Market for my first ever cookbook signing. It is so easy to make and only requires five simple ingredients. Folks raved about it. One customer who sampled it said he would never forget it.*

*Try if for yourself -- it's simply unforgettable.*

**PREP TIME:** 5 MINUTES  **TOTAL TIME:** 30 MINUTES  **SERVES:** 4

*Ingredients*

2 tablespoons extra-virgin olive oil
1 medium onion, chopped
3 pounds of tomatoes, chopped with juices
OR
2 (28 ounce) cans diced tomatoes with their juices
1 teaspoon kosher salt
¼ teaspoon freshly ground pepper

*Directions*

Heat olive oil in a stock pot over medium heat. Add chopped onions; cook until translucent and tender. Add tomatoes, then cook for about 25 minutes. Puree ingredients in a food processor until smooth. Add salt and pepper. Serve immediately.

*Chrisetta Mosley's "Simply Unforgettable Tomato Soup"
At New Seasons Market – Fisher's Landing*

# LENTIL SOUP

*A timeless classic.*

**PREP TIME:** 10 MINUTES   **TOTAL TIME:** 45 MINUTES   **SERVES:** 4

*Ingredients*

2 tablespoons extra-virgin olive oil
1 leek, thinly sliced
1 garlic clove, finely minced
1 teaspoon kosher salt
¼ teaspoon freshly ground pepper
2 teaspoons thyme
2 celery stalks, chopped
1 carrot, chopped
2 quarts vegetable broth
1 (6 ounce) can tomato paste
1 ¼ cups dried lentils

*Directions*

In a large stockpot on medium heat, sauté the leeks and garlic with the olive oil, salt, pepper, and thyme for 20 minutes until the vegetables are translucent and very tender. Add the celery and carrots and sauté for 10 more minutes. Add the vegetable stock, tomato paste, and lentils. Cover and bring to a boil. Reduce the heat and simmer over low heat until the lentils are almost tender, about 30 minutes.

# COOL FRUIT SOUP

*A cool and healthy way to enjoy fruit.*

**PREP TIME:** 5 MINUTES  **TOTAL TIME:** 65 MINUTES  **SERVES:** 6

*Ingredients*

1 cup peaches
1 cup nectarines
1 cup apricots
⅓ cup water
2 tablespoons non-fat plain yogurt
½ teaspoon ground cinnamon

**Peel, pit, and slice the fruit**

*Directions*

Place all ingredients excluding water in a food processor or blender, puree until smooth. Adjust the thickness with more or less water. Refrigerate for at least 1 hour to allow the flavors to come together. Pour the soup into chilled soup bowls. Serve immediately.

# AVOCADO TOMATO SALAD

*This recipe was inspired by Barefoot Contessa. All the ingredients of guacamole come together in a salad. The lime vinaigrette gives this salad a flavorful kick.*

**PREP TIME:** 5 MINUTES   **TOTAL TIME:** 35 MINUTES   **SERVES:** 4

*Ingredients*

### Salad

1 pint grape tomatoes, halved
1 yellow bell pepper, seeded and cut into ½-inch cubes
1 cup black beans, drained
½ cup red onion, small diced
2 tablespoons jalapeno peppers, seeded, minced (2 peppers)
½ teaspoon freshly grated lime zest
2 ripe Hass avocados, seeded, peeled, and diced into ½-inch cubes

### Lime Vinaigrette

¼ cup freshly squeezed lime juice (2 limes)
¼ cup extra-virgin olive oil
1 teaspoon kosher salt
½ teaspoon freshly ground black pepper
½ teaspoon garlic, minced
¼ teaspoon ground cayenne pepper

*Directions*

Place the tomatoes, yellow pepper, black beans, red onion, jalapeno peppers, and lime zest in a large bowl. Whisk together the lime juice, olive oil, salt, black pepper, garlic, and cayenne pepper and pour over the vegetables. Toss well.

Fold the avocados into the salad right before you're ready to serve the salad. Check the seasoning and serve at room temperature.

# WHEAT BERRY SPINACH SALAD

*Who needs croutons? The wheat berries and sliced almonds add crunch, and bonus -- are nutritionally dense. The feta cheese adds a delightful tang. This is a salad you'll want to make again and again.*

**PREP TIME:** 10 MINUTES   **TOTAL TIME:** 10 MINUTES   **SERVES:** 4

*Ingredients*

## Salad

4 cups baby spinach
1 cup wheat berries, cooked, rinsed
1 cup sliced almonds
1 red bell pepper, seeded and sliced
¼ cup feta cheese, crumbled

## Lemon Vinaigrette

½ cup extra-virgin olive oil
¼ cup freshly squeezed lemon juice (2 lemons)
1 garlic clove, minced
½ teaspoon kosher salt
¼ teaspoon freshly ground black pepper

*Directions*

### For Salad:
In large bowl, combine the spinach, wheat berries, almonds, and feta cheese. Drizzle with lemon vinaigrette. Serve immediately or make ahead of time keeping the dressing separate. Combine when ready to serve.

### For Lemon Vinaigrette:
In salad dressing shaker bottle add lemon juice, olive oil, salt, pepper, and garlic. Shake until ingredients are mixed.

# GREEK SALAD

*I love Greek cuisine. This is one of my favorite salads. Use Greek oregano and Greek feta - they give the salad a distinct Greekness.*

**PREP TIME:** 20 MINUTES  **TOTAL TIME:** 20 MINUTES  **SERVES** 4

*Ingredients*

### Salad

1 pint cherry or grape tomatoes, halved
1 small red onion, diced
1 cucumber, peeled, halved, and thinly sliced
½ cup Greek feta cheese, crumbled
½ cup Kalamata olives, pitted and halved

### Vinaigrette

½ cup extra-virgin olive oil
¼ cup freshly squeezed lemon juice (2 lemons)
¼ teaspoon Greek oregano
½ teaspoon kosher salt
¼ teaspoon freshly ground black pepper

*Directions*

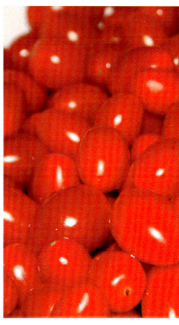

In salad dressing shaker bottle add olive oil, lemon juice, Greek oregano, salt, and pepper  Shake until ingredients are mixed. Set aside.

Place tomatoes, red onion, cucumbers, feta cheese, and Kalamata olives in large bowl.  Gently toss ingredients together. Just before serving, pour the vinaigrette over the salad and serve.

*If you're not going to eat the salad right away, store vinaigrette and salad separately in your fridge for up to 24 hours and then toss right before serving.*

# CAPRESE SALAD

*Simple, fresh Italian classic.*

**PREP TIME:** 5 MINUTES   **TOTAL TIME:** 5 MINUTES   **SERVES:** 4

*Ingredients*

3 whole ripe tomatoes, sliced thick
12 ounces, mozzarella cheese, sliced thick
Fresh basil leaves
Extra-virgin olive oil
Kosher salt to taste
Freshly ground black pepper to taste

*Directions*

Arrange tomato and mozzarella slices on a platter. Arrange basil leaves between the slices. Drizzle olive oil over the top of the salad, getting a little bit on each slice. End with a sprinkling of kosher salt and black pepper. Serve.

*For a sweet touch Instead of olive oil drizzle with Balsamic vinegar*

# GREEN BEAN & POTATO SALAD

*I fell in love with this salad with the first bite I took. It was like springtime in my mouth. The fresh garden vegetables are highlighted by a tangy, lemony balsamic vinaigrette.*

**PREP TIME**: 15 MINUTES   **TOTAL TIME:** 45 MINUTES   **SERVES:** 6

*Ingredients*

## Salad

1 ½ pounds small red potatoes
1 pound fresh green beans, trimmed
1 small red onion, diced
¼ cup fresh basil, chopped

## Balsamic Vinaigrette

½ cup extra-virgin olive oil
¼ cup balsamic vinegar
2 tablespoons Dijon mustard
2 tablespoons freshly squeezed lemon juice
1 teaspoon kosher salt
¼ teaspoon freshly ground black pepper
Dash of Worcestershire sauce
1 garlic clove, minced

*Directions*

Arrange potatoes in steamer basket over boiling water; cover and steam 20 minutes or until tender. Place in a large serving bowl. Arrange beans in steamer basket over boiling water, cover and steam 10 minutes or until tender, but still a bit crisp.  Try not to overcook.

Meanwhile, make vinaigrette. Combine all ingredients in a salad shaker bottle or covered jar and shake vigorously.

Cut potatoes in half, add beans, onion, and basil. Drizzle with balsamic vinaigrette and gently combine. Serve immediately or cover and chill.

# ANY SEASON FRUIT SALAD

*For the freshest tasting salads, choose fruit that are at the peak of their season. Here's a few fruit combinations, but the choices are unlimited. Be creative and have fun!*

**PREP TIME:** 5 MINUTES  **TOTAL TIME:** 5 MINUTES  **SERVES:** 2

*Ingredients*

### Spring:
1 cup sliced strawberries
1 cup seedless grapes
1 small kiwi, peeled and sliced

### Summer:
1 cup honeydew melon, peeled, seeded, and diced
1 cup cantaloupe, peeled, seeded, and diced
1 ½ cups seedless watermelon, diced

OR

1 cup blueberries
2 small peaches, peeled, pitted, and sliced
½ teaspoon cinnamon

### Fall:
1 apple, cored and sliced
1 cup fresh cranberries
¼ cup pomegranate berries
1 pear, peeled, cored,
A good squeeze of lemon juice
½ teaspoon cinnamon

### Winter:
1 orange, peeled and sectioned
1 mango, peeled, seeded, and sliced
1 cup fresh pineapple, peeled, cored, and cut in chunks
A good squeeze of lime juice

*Directions*

In medium bowl, toss fruit together gently. If salad recipe calls for it, drizzle with lemon or lime juice and sprinkle with cinnamon. Serve immediately.

# CLASSICS

MACARONI & CHEESE

OVEN-FRIED CHICKEN STRIPS

CHILI

# MACARONI & CHEESE

*I'd be remiss to leave this recipe out. There is no substitute for homemade mac and cheese -- the ultimate American comfort food.*

**PREP TIME:** 15 MINUTES   **TOTAL TIME:** 1 HOUR   **SERVES:** 6 - 8

*Ingredients*

1 pound elbow macaroni
3 cups milk
8 tablespoons (1 stick) unsalted butter
½ cup all-purpose flour
2 cups extra-sharp cheddar cheese, shredded
1 teaspoon kosher salt
½ teaspoon freshly ground black pepper
½ teaspoon ground nutmeg
1 cup parmesan cheese, grated

*Directions*

Preheat the oven to 375 degrees.

Cook the pasta according to package instructions; drain and reserve.

In a large sauce pan, melt the butter.  Then whisk in the flour and continue to whisk for about 5 minutes. Make sure it's free of lumps. Gradually add milk and make sure to heat until nice and creamy. Do not boil. Remove from heat. Stir in extra-sharp cheddar, salt, pepper, and nutmeg. Add the cooked macaroni and stir until blended. Spoon the macaroni and cheese into a 3-quart baking dish. Top with parmesan cheese.

Bake uncovered for 30 to 35 minutes, or until the sauce is bubbly and the macaroni is browned on the top. Remove from oven and allow to rest for ten minutes before serving. Enjoy!

# OVEN-FRIED CHICKEN STRIPS

*Soaking the chicken in buttermilk makes the chicken incredibly tender and juicy. Oven-frying is a great, tasty alternative to traditional deep fried. Enjoy!*

**PREP TIME:** 5 MINUTES  **TOTAL TIME:** 30 MINUTES  **SERVES:** 4

*Ingredients*

Canola oil (just enough to thinly coat a baking sheet)
1 pound boneless, skinless chicken breasts
½ cup buttermilk
1 cup crumbs (bread or panko)
1½ teaspoon kosher salt
1 teaspoon paprika
½ teaspoon garlic powder
½ teaspoon freshly ground black pepper

*Directions*

Preheat the oven to 400 degrees. Meanwhile, lightly coat a baking sheet with oil.

Cut the chicken breasts into strips approximately ½-inch wide. Place chicken strips in a shallow dish and cover with buttermilk. Soak in the fridge for at least 15 minutes.

While the strips are soaking, combine the crumbs and seasonings in a large plastic bag. Drain the excess buttermilk from the chicken strips. Add the strips, a few at a time, to the crumb mixture and shake to coat thoroughly. Remove and place on the baking sheet; cook for 15 – 20 minutes turning once (The cooking time will vary depending on thickness of strips). Use a meat thermometer to verify the chicken has reached 165°F. Serve hot from the oven.

# CHILI

*Perfectly spicy and hearty. This chili is umm, umm, umm good.*

**PREP TIME:** 15 MIN   **TOTAL TIME:** 1 HR, 15 MIN   **SERVES:** 6 - 8

*Ingredients*

4 tablespoons canola oil
1 ½ pounds lean ground beef
2 teaspoons kosher salt
½ teaspoon freshly ground black pepper
1 yellow onion, chopped
4 garlic cloves, minced
2 (14.5 ounce) cans low-sodium whole peeled tomatoes, chopped, juice reserved
1 (12 ounce) can tomato paste
2 ½ teaspoons chili powder
1 teaspoon cayenne pepper
1 teaspoon ground cumin
1 cup each black and red beans, cooked or canned, rinsed and drained
Water

*Directions*

Heat oil in a large Dutch oven or large pot over high heat. Season the ground beef with salt and pepper, and sauté until browned on all sides. Transfer the ground beef to a plate and remove all but 3 tablespoons of the fat from the pan. Add the onions to the pan and cook until soft. Add the garlic and cook for 2 minutes.

Stir in tomatoes and tomato paste. Season with chili powder, cayenne pepper, and ground cumin. Bring to a boil over high heat. Reduce heat to medium low. Return ground beef to pot. Cover, and simmer for 25-30 minutes, stirring occasionally. Add a little water if needed to keep from sticking.

Stir in beans. You can add the reserved tomato juice if more liquid is needed. Continue to simmer for an additional 30 minutes.

**Serve with any combination:**
Sour cream
Grated cheddar
Diced tomato
Baked tortilla chips (page 47)

# DIPS & SPREADS

GUACAMOLE

FRESH SALSA

SMOKY BEAN DIP

HUMMUS

ITALIAN DRESSING

RANCH DRESSING

STRAWBERRY JAM

YOGURT BERRY SPREAD

# GUACAMOLE

**PREP TIME:** 5 MINUTES   **TOTAL TIME:** 5 MINUTES   **SERVES:** 6

*Ingredients*

3 Haas avocados, halved, seeded and peeled
1 lime, juiced
½ teaspoon kosher salt
⅛ teaspoon cayenne pepper
¼ medium red onion, diced
1 Roma tomato, seeded and diced
1 big handful fresh cilantro leaves, finely chopped
Baked tortilla chips (page 47) for serving, optional

*Directions*

Halve and pit the avocados, then scoop out the flesh with a tablespoon into a mixing bowl. Mash the avocados with a fork, leaving them still a bit chunky. Add the remaining ingredients, and fold everything together to gently mix.

Lay a piece of plastic wrap right on the surface of the guacamole so it doesn't brown and refrigerate for at least 1 hour before serving.

# FRESH SALSA

*My girlfriend, Patricia Rojas whipped up this fresh salsa recipe when I was at her house for a Mexican fiesta. I was in awe at how simple it is to make and how fresh and delicious it tastes. It's become a staple at my house.*

*I suggest you make it several hours ahead of time to allow the flavors to develop.*

**PREP TIME:** 10 MINUTES  **TOTAL TIME:** 2 HOURS, 10 MINUTES  **SERVES:** 4

*Ingredients*

6 Roma tomatoes, whole
2 jalapenos red or green, whole (cut and clean out seeds for less spice)
A handful of cilantro
1 garlic clove, peeled
Juice from ½ a lime
Big pinch of Kosher salt

*Directions*

Rinse tomatoes and jalapenos. Place tomatoes and jalapenos in microwave-safe dish. Microwave for 4-6 minutes until tomatoes and jalapenos are soft. Meanwhile, in a food processor pulse cilantro and garlic. Add softened tomatoes, jalapenos, lime juice, and salt to food processor. Puree all ingredients until well blended 1-2 minutes. Pour in dish and place in fridge for at least two hours (the longer the better it gives time for the flavors to develop) before serving.

# SMOKY BEAN DIP

**PREP TIME:** 5 MINUTES  **TOTAL TIME:** 25 MINUTES  **SERVES:** 6

*Ingredients*

1 cup scallions, chopped
Kosher salt to taste
½ cup cilantro, chopped
1 tablespoon ground cumin
1 tablespoon paprika
1 tablespoon extra-virgin olive oil
2 cups black beans, cooked and drained
6 tablespoons freshly squeezed lime juice (2 limes)

*Directions*

In a skillet over medium heat, add oil, scallions, and spices. Let flavors combine together for about 10 minutes. In a food processor, purée black beans with cilantro.  Add scallions and spices to food processor and purée together. Add lime juice and salt. Serve slightly chilled with fresh vegetables, baked tortilla chips (page 47) or pita bread.

# HUMMUS

**PREP TIME:** 5 MINUTES   **TOTAL TIME:** 25 MINUTES   **SERVES:** 6

*Ingredients*

2 cups garbanzo beans (chickpeas), drained, liquid reserved
4 garlic cloves
1½ teaspoons kosher salt
⅓ cup tahini (sesame paste)
6 tablespoons freshly squeezed lemon juice (2 lemons)
2 tablespoons liquid from the chickpeas
8 dashes hot sauce

*Directions*

Drain chickpeas and reserve liquid. Place drained chickpeas and rest of ingredients in a blender or food processor.  Blend on low until smooth and thoroughly mixed, 3-5 minutes, adding reserved chickpea liquid as needed to form a thick paste. Season to taste. Serve chilled with fresh vegetables, warm pita bread, or pita chips.

# ITALIAN DRESSING

**PREP TIME:** 5 MINUTES  **TOTAL TIME:** 5 MINUTES  **SERVES:** 6

*Ingredients*

6 tablespoons olive oil
2 tablespoons white wine vinegar
2 tablespoons fresh parsley, chopped
1 tablespoon fresh lemon juice
2 garlic cloves, chopped
1 teaspoon dried basil, crumbled
¼ teaspoon dried crushed red pepper
Pinch of dried oregano
Kosher salt to taste
Freshly ground black pepper to taste

*Directions*

Mix all ingredients together in a salad shaker bottle. Season to taste with salt and pepper. Cover. Can be refrigerated for up to one week.

# RANCH DRESSING

**PREP TIME:** 5 MINUTES    **TOTAL TIME:** 25 MINUTES    **SERVES:** 6

*Ingredients*

1 cup buttermilk
½ cup mayonnaise
1 teaspoon freshly squeezed lemon juice
⅛ teaspoon paprika
¼ teaspoon mustard powder
1 tablespoon fresh parsley, chopped
1 teaspoon fresh chives, chopped
1 teaspoon fresh dill, chopped
½ teaspoon Kosher salt
⅛ teaspoon freshly ground black pepper

*Directions*

In a medium bowl, using wire whisk, whisk together the buttermilk and mayonnaise until well combined. Add lemon juice, paprika, mustard powder, and herbs. Season to taste with salt and pepper. Cover.  Can be refrigerated for up to one week.

# STRAWBERRY JAM

*Clark College's "Food and Your Health" instructor, Kristen Myklebust uses this reduced-sugar recipe every summer using the berries she picks with her kids. She says "Fresh, ripe, in-season fruit is the best way to go here. And usually the berries we buy are the most hideous looking but taste the best. The big red strawberries at the grocery store pale next to the tiny, bright red misshapen yet perfectly flavored farm berries. It's not all about looks on the berry farm."*

**PREP TIME:** 5 MINUTES   **TOTAL TIME:** 24 HOURS   **MAKES:** ABOUT 5 PINTS

*Ingredients*

4 cups berries
2 cups sugar
1 tablespoon lemon juice
1 packet SURE JELL Premium Fruit Pectin  (pink box "no sugar needed")
Mason jars

*Directions*

Wash berries well under cold water, then drain. If using strawberries, cut off tops. Mash berries with potato masher (or bottom of glass jar) until fairly well mashed but still with some small chunks of berries.

Mix fresh lemon juice, and one packet of SURE JELL pectin with sugar in a large saucepan. Mix really well to incorporate the sugar with the pectin. Add one cup of water to sugar-pectin mixture. Bring mixture to boil on medium-high heat, stirring constantly. Boil and stir 1 minute. Remove from heat.

Add mixture to berries quickly and stir 1 minute or until thoroughly mixed. Pour into prepared jars leaving ½ inch space at top for expansion during freezing; cover.

Let stand at room temperature 24 hours until set. Refrigerate up to 3 weeks. Otherwise, store in freezer for up to 1 year. Thaw in refrigerator.

# YOGURT BERRY SPREAD

*This spread is great on whole grain bread, bagels, waffles, or even pancakes.*

**PREP TIME:** 5 MINUTES   **TOTAL TIME:** 10 MINUTES   **MAKES:** 2 CUPS

*Ingredients*

1 cup fresh strawberries, chopped
½ cup blueberries, chopped
½ cup blackberries, chopped
½ cup nonfat plain yogurt
A good squeeze of fresh lemon juice

*Directions*

In a blender or food processor, puree the berries, yogurt, and lemon juice a few seconds until smooth. This is best made several hours ahead of time so that flavors can blend.

You may substitute frozen berries, but make sure to thaw them before measuring.

# SWEET SENSATIONS

ORANGE GRANITA

FROZEN CHOCOLATE BANANAS

BERRY GRANOLA PARFAIT

OATMEAL CRANBERRY COOKIES

# ORANGE GRANITA

*A homemade orange slushie. Enough said.*

**PREP TIME:** 5 MINUTES   **TOTAL TIME:** 1 HR, 30 MIN   **MAKES:** 2

*Ingredients*

6 large oranges, juiced
A good squeeze of lemon or lime juice

*Directions*

Mix the orange juice and lemon or lime juice. Pour into a freezer bag. Set in the freezer. Every 20 to 30 minutes remove and break the frozen juice with a fork. Repeat at least four more times. Eat right away or freeze for up to 3 weeks.

# FROZEN CHOCOLATE BANANAS

*Chocolate dipped bananas. Yum!*

**PREP TIME**: 5 MINUTES   **TOTAL TIME:** 1 HR, 10 MIN   **MAKES:** 8 -12

*Ingredients*

4 bananas
Popsicle sticks or wooden skewers
10 ounces milk or dark chocolate

*Directions*

Line a baking sheet with parchment paper. Peel the bananas. Cut each banana diagonally into 4 pieces. Put a stick or skewer into each banana bite. Place on the lined baking sheet. Place into freezer for an hour  or until completely frozen. Bring a small pan of water to simmer gently. Set a bowl over the top of the pan, checking that the bottom of the bowl is not touching the  water in the pan. Chop the chocolate and place into the bowl. Once the chocolate  starts melting stir into a smooth sauce.  Remove banana bites from freezer. Dip banana bites into the chocolate to coat. Place banana bites back on lined baking sheet. Freeze. Once frozen, enjoy right away or store in freezer bags.

**For a twist, try these:**

**Coconut**
*Roll the dipped chocolate bites in unsweetened coconut flakes*

**Peanut**
*Sprinkle chopped peanuts over the dipped chocolate bites*

# BERRY GRANOLA PARFAIT

*A creamy, crunchy delight. Using a combination of whatever fresh berries are in season or frozen will work fine too. If using frozen berries, thaw in the microwave for about a minute prior to use.*

**PREP TIME:** 5 MINUTES   **TOTAL TIME:** 5 MINUTES   **MAKES:** 1

*Ingredients*

¾ cup sliced strawberries
¾ cup blueberries, blackberries, or raspberries – your choice
⅔ cup plain Greek yogurt
2 tablespoons Granola Fruit Nut Crunch (page 73)
1 teaspoon chia, flax, or hemp seeds

*Directions*

Spoon ⅓ cup yogurt in the bottom of a glass and smooth the top. Add 1 tablespoon berry mixture, ⅓ tablespoon seeds and 1 tablespoon granola. Repeat the layers and eat right away, or chill in refrigerator for up to a day.

# OATMEAL CRANBERRY COOKIES

*These cookies are easy to make and will taste much better than store-bought.*

**PREP TIME:** 10 MINUTES   **TOTAL TIME:** 20 MINUTES   **MAKES:** 4 DOZEN

*Ingredients*

½ cup (1 stick) plus 6 tablespoons butter, softened
¾ cup firmly packed brown sugar
½ cup raw cane sugar or natural cane sugar
2 eggs
1 teaspoon vanilla
1½ cups whole wheat pastry flour
1 teaspoon baking soda
1 teaspoon ground cinnamon
½ teaspoon salt, optional
3 cups old fashioned oats (uncooked)
1 cup dried cranberries
1 cup unsweetened coconut flakes

> *Be creative and add your favorite mix-ins to the cookies – any kind of dried fruit, nuts or chocolate combination will work. If using these options omit the cinnamon.*

*Directions*

Heat oven to 350 degrees. Combine flour, baking soda, cinnamon, and salt in small bowl. In large bowl, beat butter and sugars on medium speed of electric mixer until creamy. Add eggs and vanilla; beat well. Gradually beat in flour mixture. Add oats and cranberries; mix well.

Drop dough by rounded tablespoonfuls onto ungreased cookie sheets. Bake 8 to 10 minutes or until light golden brown. Cool 1 minute on cookie sheets; remove to wire rack. Cool completely. Store tightly covered.

**For bars:** Press dough onto bottom of ungreased 13 x 9-inch baking pan. Bake 30 to 35 minutes or until light golden brown. Cool completely in pan on wire rack. Cut into bars. Store tightly covered.

> *Cookies can be enjoyed if you watch the amount and type of cookies you eat. These cookies are made with whole oats and whole wheat flour so they have some better qualities than packaged cookies you can buy which tend to be high in fat, sugar, and who knows what else!*

# EAT

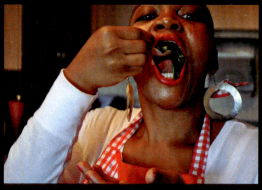

# INDEX

Asparagus, Garlic Roasted, 85
Avocado
  Avocado Tomato Salad, 96-97
  Guacamole, 112
  Santa Fe Chicken Wraps, 56
Bananas, Frozen Chocolate, 123
Basics
  Beans, how to cook, 32-33
  Grains, how to cook, 34-35
  Hard-boiled Eggs, 41
  Olive Oil Drizzle, 40
  Tomato Sauce, 38
  Vegetable Stock, 36-37
  Vinaigrettes, 39
Bean(s), see also Lentil(s)
  Chili, 108 -109
  Green Bean & Potato Salad, 102
  Hummus, 115
  Mexican Rice Bowl, 61
  Santa Fe Chicken Wraps, 56
  Smoky Bean Dip, 114
  Spicy Roasted Chickpeas, 44-45
  Veggie Wrap, 58
Berries
  Berry Granola Parfait, 124
  Fruit Kebabs, 51
Bowls
  Fruit Seed Wheat Berry, 72
  Greek Quinoa, 62
  Mexican Rice, 61
  Vegetable Fried Rice, 60
Brussels Sprouts, Roasted, 86
Cauliflower, Parmesan Roasted, 83
Collard Greens, Sautéed, 87
Chia seeds
  Berry Granola Parfait, 124
  Blueberry Banana Kale Smoothie, 66
  Fruit Seed Wheat Berry Bowl, 72
  Go Green Drink, 67
Chicken
  Greek Wraps, 57
  Lettuce Wraps, 59
  Oven-Fried Chicken Strips, 107
  Santa Fe Chicken Wraps, 56
Chickpeas
  Hummus, 115
  Spicy Roasted Chickpeas, 44
Chili, 108

Chips
  Baked Tortilla Chips, 47
  Kale Chips, 46
Chocolate
  Frozen Chocolate Bananas, 123
Cranberries
  Granola Fruit Nut Crunch, 73
  Fruit Seed Wheat Berry Bowl, 72
  Oatmeal Cranberry Cookies, 125
Dates
  Cashew Energy Bars, 52
  Chocolate Coconut Energy Bars, 53
Eggs
  Classic Omelette, 70-71
  Hard-boiled Eggs, 41
  Open-Faced Egg Sandwich, 68-69
Feta Cheese
  Greek Wraps, 57
  Greek Salad, 99
  Wheat Berry Spinach Salad, 98
  Zucchini Mushroom Tacos, 63
Fresh Salsa, 113
Granola Fruit Nut Crunch, 73
Grocery Shopping
  Grocery List, 19
  Planning, 18
  Tips, 21
Honey
  Granola Fruit Nut Crunch, 73
  Teriyaki Sauce, 59
Jam
  Strawberry, 118
Kale
  Blueberry Banana Kale Smoothie, 66
  Go Green Drink, 67
  Kale Chips, 46
Kalamata Olives
  Greek Quinoa Bowl, 62
  Greek Salad, 99
  Greek Wraps, 57
Kitchen
  Essentials, 22-23
  Tips, 25-27
  Tools, 24
Lentil(s)
  how to cook, 33
  Lentil soup, 94

Macaroni and Cheese, 106
Oats
　how to cook, 34-35
　Granola Fruit Nut Crunch, 73
　Oatmeal Cranberry Cookies, 125
　Steel Cut Oatmeal, 74
Oatmeal Cranberry Cookies, 125
Oatmeal, Steel Cut, 74
Omelette, Classic
　Cheese, 71
　Herb, 71
　Southwestern, 71
　Vegetable, 71
Orange Granita, 122
Peppers, Roasted, 84
Quinoa
　how to cook, 34-35
　Greek Quinoa Bowl, 62
　Veggie Wrap, 58
Salad dressings, see also Vinaigrettes
　Balsamic, 39
　Greek, 99
　Italian, 116
　Lemon, 39, 98
　Lime, 96
　Ranch, 117
Salads
　Avocado Tomato Salad, 96-97
　Caprese, 100
　Fruit Salad, Any Season, 103
　Greek, 99
　Green Bean & Potato, 102
　Wheat Berry Spinach Salad, 98
Smoothie, Blueberry Banana Kale, 66
Snacks
　Baked Tortilla Chips, 47
　Brown Bag Popcorn, 48
　Cashew Energy Bars, 52
　Chocolate Coconut Energy Bars, 53
　Fresh Vegetable Kebabs, 50
　Fruit Kebabs, 51
　Kale Chips, 46
　Spicy Roasted Chickpeas, 44
Spinach
　Santa Fe Chicken Wraps, 56
　Veggie Wraps, 58
　Wheat Berry Spinach Salad, 98
Soup
　Cool Fruit, 95
　Lentil, 94
　Simply Unforgettable Tomato, 92-93
　Sweet Potato Bisque, 90 -91
Strawberry
　Jam, 118

Sweet Potatoes
　Baked, 80
　Bisque, 90-91
　Fries, 78 -79
Tacos
　Zucchini Mushroom, 63
Teriyaki Sauce, 59
Tomatoes
　Avocado Tomato Salad, 96-97
　Caprese Salad, 100
　Chili, 108
　Fresh Salsa, 113
　Greek Quinoa Bowl, 62
　Greek Salad, 99
　Open-Faced Egg Sandwich, 68
　Plum, Roasted, 82
　Simply Unforgettable Tomato Soup. 92-93
　Tomato Sauce, 38
Tortillas
　Baked Tortilla Chips, 47
　Greek Wraps, 57
　Santa Fe Chicken Wraps, 56
　Veggie Wraps, 58
　Zucchini Mushroom Tacos, 63
Vinaigrettes
　Balsamic, 39
　Greek, 99
　Lemon, 39,98
　Lime, 96
Wheat berries
　how to cook, 35
　Fruit Seed Wheat Berry Bowl, 72
　Wheat Berry Spinach Salad, 98
Wraps
　Greek, 57
　Lettuce, 59
　Santa Fe Chicken, 56
　Veggie, 58
Yogurt
　Blueberry Banana Kale Smoothie, 66
　Berry Spread, 119
　Fruit Seed Wheat Berry Bowl, 72
Zucchini Mushroom Tacos, 63

# Congrats
from Seattle University Professor

"Chrisetta, I know I have told you this before, but I want to tell you again how immensely proud I am of your work and you joie de vivre. Professors go on teaching because of stories such as yours. What fabulous creativity, drive, and entrepreneurship you have achieved. Chrisetta Mosley, author, blogger, speaker, culinary goddess - Congratulations!"

- Sonora Jha
Associate Professor of Journalism
Chair, Department of Communication